GIRLS ONLY

ONLY

HOW TO
SURVIVE
(ALMOST)
ANYTHING!

BUSTER BOOKS

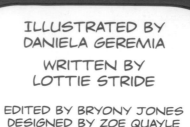

ILLUSTRATED BY
DANIELA GEREMIA
WRITTEN BY
LOTTIE STRIDE

EDITED BY BRYONY JONES
DESIGNED BY ZOE QUAYLE

DISCLAIMER
The publisher and author disclaim, as far as is
legally permissible, all liability for accidents,
or injuries or loss that may occur as a result
of information or instructions given in this book.

The hints and tips in this book are intended for
practice purposes only. Use your best common sense
at all times – particularly when using heat or sharp objects.
Always remember to ask a responsible adult for
assistance and take their advice whenever necessary.

First published in Great Britain in 2012 by Buster Books,
an imprint of Michael O'Mara Books Limited,
9 Lion Yard, Tremadoc Road, London SW4 7NQ

www.busterbooks.co.uk

A CIP catalogue record for this book is available from the British Library.

ISBN: 978-1-907151-99-6

1 3 5 7 9 10 8 6 4 2

Papers used by Michael O'Mara Books are natural, recyclable products
made from wood grown in sustainable forests. The manufacturing processes
conform to the environmental regulations of the country of origin.

This book was printed in April 2012 by Shenzhen Wing King Tong Paper Products Co. Ltd.,
Shenzhen, Guangdong, China.

CONTENTS

WARNING!

NOT READING THIS BOOK COULD SERIOUSLY CRAMP YOUR STYLE.

HOW WOULD YOU COPE IF YOU WERE ASKED TO MAKE A SPEECH TO A ROOM FULL OF PEOPLE? WHAT WOULD YOU DO IF YOU WERE FACED WITH A ZOMBIE ATTACK? HOW WOULD YOU REACT IF YOU HAD A HUGE FIGHT WITH YOUR BEST FRIEND?

THIS FABULOUS BOOK WILL SHOW YOU HOW TO SURVIVE ANYTHING LIFE THROWS AT YOU IN THE MOST STYLISH WAY POSSIBLE.

WHETHER IT'S THE LITTLE THINGS IN LIFE, LIKE CHOOSING THE RIGHT PAIR OF SUNGLASSES, OR THE STRANGER THINGS, SUCH AS ENCOUNTERING VAMPIRES, THIS BOOK WILL TELL YOU WHAT TO DO, AND HOW TO DO IT WITH STYLE.

GET READY TO BE SUPER-STYLISH

BEING A STYLE SENSATION ISN'T JUST ABOUT HOW YOU LOOK, IT'S ABOUT HAVING THE CONFIDENCE TO BE YOURSELF, AND MAKING OTHERS FEEL GREAT ABOUT THEMSELVES, TOO.

BE A FANTASTIC FRIEND

- MAKE YOUR FRIENDS SMILE BY PAYING THEM COMPLIMENTS.

- BE TRUSTWORTHY, NOT A GOSSIP. KEEP OTHER PEOPLE'S SECRETS SECRET.

- IF A FRIEND IS FEELING DOWN, TAKE NOTICE AND TRY TO CHEER HER UP.

- REMEMBER FRIENDS' BIRTHDAYS, AND SURPRISE THEM WITH CARDS.

BE UTTERLY FABULOUS

- DON'T FOLLOW THE CROWD - CREATE YOUR OWN LOOK.

- ACT CONFIDENT, EVEN IF YOU DON'T FEEL CONFIDENT INSIDE.

- PUT YOUR BEST INTO EVERYTHING YOU DO, EVEN IF IT'S SOMETHING YOU'RE DREADING.

- TAKE A LEAP - SOMETIMES THE MOST REWARDING THINGS ARE THE THINGS THAT SEEM THE SCARIEST WHEN YOU START, SUCH AS TRYING OUT FOR THE FOOTBALL TEAM.

SO WHAT ARE YOU WAITING FOR? TURN THE PAGE AND READ, LEARN - AND ENJOY!

HOW TO SURVIVE A BFF FIGHT

ALL FRIENDS FALL OUT SOMETIMES. HERE'S A GUIDE TO THE DOS AND DON'TS OF GETTING THROUGH EVEN THE BIGGEST BUST-UP.

REVENGE IS SATISFYING ... BUT NOT REALLY THE ANSWER.

WE'RE NOT TALKING TO HER. SHE'S NOT OUR FRIEND ANY MORE.

BESIDES, REVENGE CAN WORK BOTH WAYS!

HEY, WHERE ARE YOU ALL GOING?

SULKING IS **SO** NOT A GOOD LOOK.

AND BEING A DRAMA QUEEN WON'T SORT ANYTHING OUT.

BESIDES, JUST THINK ABOUT ALL THE FUN YOU'VE HAD TOGETHER ...

HE'S SO CUTE!

... AND ALL THE SECRETS YOU'VE SHARED.

IS IT REALLY WORTH LOSING A FRIEND? IS IT TIME TO MAKE UP INSTEAD?

FIRST, WHY NOT ARRANGE TO MEET UP IN ONE OF YOUR FAVOURITE PLACES?

THERE ARE TWO SIDES TO EVERY STORY, SO LISTEN TO EACH OTHER. IF IT HELPS, GET A REFEREE ALONG.

YOU GET THREE MINUTES EACH. NO INTERRUPTING.

IF YOU WERE WRONG, ADMIT IT. SHOW HER YOU'RE SORRY.

IF **SHE** WAS WRONG, ACCEPT HER APOLOGY AND BE GRACIOUS.

LET'S NEVER FALL OUT AGAIN!

IF YOU FIND THAT YOU WERE **BOTH** WRONG, THERE'S ONLY ONE THING TO DO ... LAUGH.

IT'S MUCH MORE FUN TO BE FRIENDS THAN ENEMIES.

WE'RE BOTH IDIOTS!

HERE ARE SOME TOP TIPS TO HELP YOU STORM STRAIGHT THROUGH TRIALS, AND ON TO THE TEAM.

1. DO THREE THINGS IN THE WEEK BEFORE THE TRIALS.

PRACTISE ...

... PRACTISE ...

... AND PRACTISE!

2. GET AN EARLY NIGHT BEFORE THE TRIALS.

3. WARM-UPS WILL HELP YOUR GAME, SO GET TO TRIALS NICE AND EARLY.

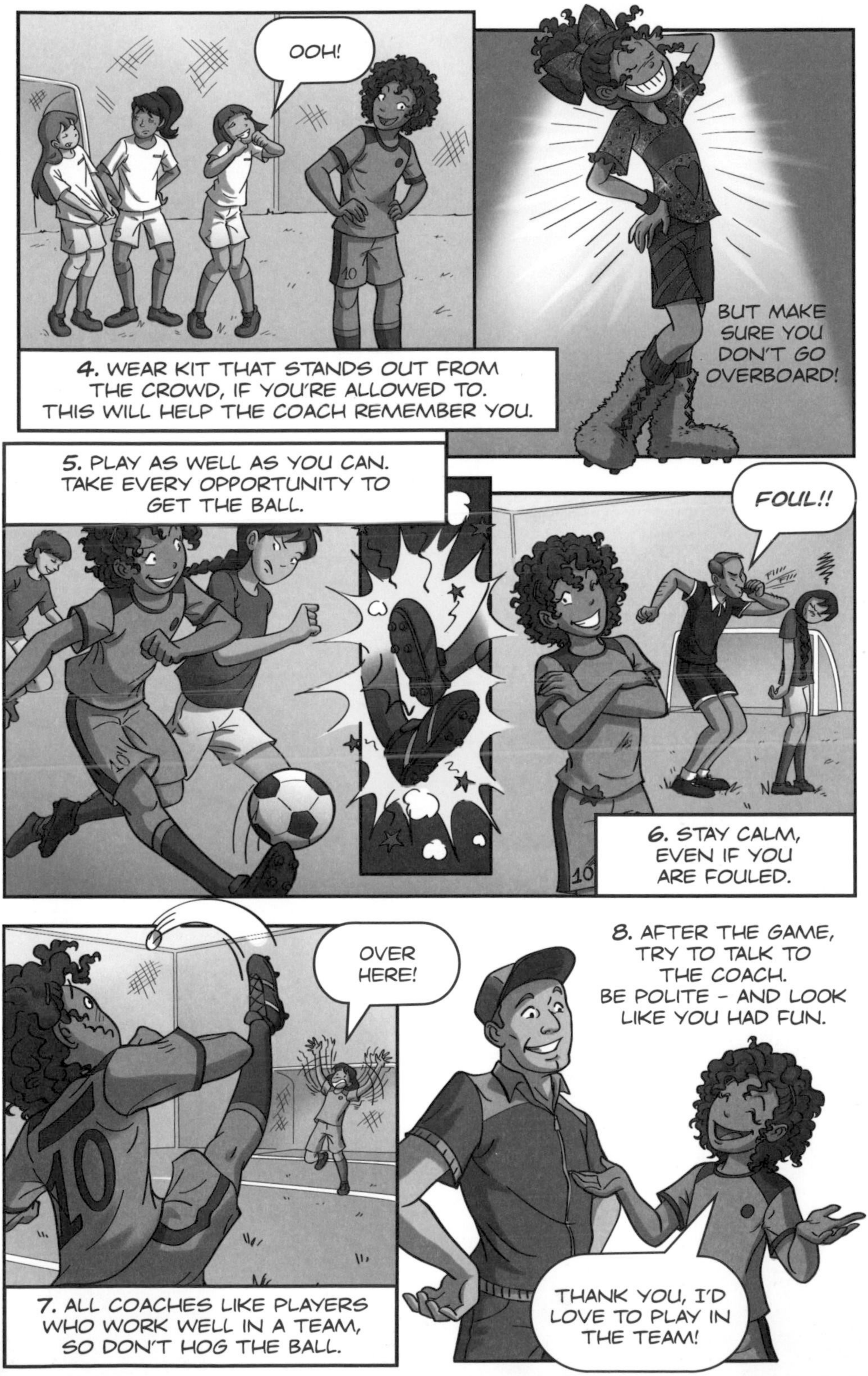
OOH!
4. WEAR KIT THAT STANDS OUT FROM THE CROWD, IF YOU'RE ALLOWED TO. THIS WILL HELP THE COACH REMEMBER YOU.
BUT MAKE SURE YOU DON'T GO OVERBOARD!
5. PLAY AS WELL AS YOU CAN. TAKE EVERY OPPORTUNITY TO GET THE BALL.
FOUL!!
6. STAY CALM, EVEN IF YOU ARE FOULED.
OVER HERE!
7. ALL COACHES LIKE PLAYERS WHO WORK WELL IN A TEAM, SO DON'T HOG THE BALL.
8. AFTER THE GAME, TRY TO TALK TO THE COACH. BE POLITE – AND LOOK LIKE YOU HAD FUN.
THANK YOU, I'D LOVE TO PLAY IN THE TEAM!

HOW TO SURVIVE A BREAKOUT

EVER WANTED TO BE ONE OF THOSE GIRLS WITH GORGEOUS, GLOWING SKIN?

IS THE REALITY RATHER DIFFERENT? DON'T PANIC! HERE'S HOW TO SURVIVE A BREAKOUT AND GET THE SKIN OF YOUR DREAMS.

WASH YOUR FACE AND KEEP IT CLEAN, SO YOUR SPOTS DON'T GET ANY WORSE.

YAWN!

ALWAYS TAKE OFF YOUR MAKE-UP BEFORE BED.

WHEN YOU TREAT YOUR SPOTS, DAB ON SOME SPOT CREAM AND THEN LEAVE THEM WELL ALONE.

NEVER, *EVER* SQUEEZE A SPOT!

HERE ARE SOME TOP TIPS TO TRY TO AVOID A BREAKOUT IN THE FIRST PLACE.

MOISTURIZE WHENEVER YOUR SKIN FEELS DRY, EVEN IF IT'S SPOTTY ...

... BUT PICK THE RIGHT MOISTURIZER FOR YOUR SENSITIVE, DRY OR OILY SKIN.

IT'S IMPORTANT TO EAT HEALTHILY. WHAT YOU PUT INSIDE SHOWS ON THE OUTSIDE, AND MIGHT HELP TO REDUCE THE CHANCE OF A BREAKOUT.

A BIT OF FRESH AIR IS GOOD FOR YOUR SKIN.

BUT DON'T FORGET TO TAKE CARE IN THE SUN.

CHOOSE AN OIL-FREE SUN CREAM IF YOUR SKIN IS GREASY AND SPOT-PRONE.

EXERCISE WILL HELP TO GIVE YOUR SKIN A GLOW.

AND IF YOU DON'T LIKE SPORT, YOU CAN FIND OTHER WAYS TO GET YOURSELF MOVING.

EIGHT HOURS OF SLEEP IS GOOD FOR SKIN.

BUT DON'T FORGET THAT SOMETIMES, JUST SOMETIMES, IT'S OK TO BREAK THE RULES!

HOW TO SHOW YOU'RE SORRY

SOMETIMES, SAYING SORRY TO A FRIEND JUST DOESN'T SEEM ENOUGH.

THAT'S WHEN A SMALL GIFT CAN HELP. WHAT WOULD SHE REALLY LIKE AS A PRESENT?

LIP BALM!

MAKE IT YOURSELF, TO SHOW YOU'RE REALLY SORRY. HERE'S WHAT YOU NEED:

1 TABLESPOON OF PETROLEUM JELLY

1 SMALL TEASPOON OF RUNNY HONEY

STIR THEM TOGETHER UNTIL THE BALM LOOKS SMOOTH. THEN PUT THE MIXTURE IN A SMALL JAR.

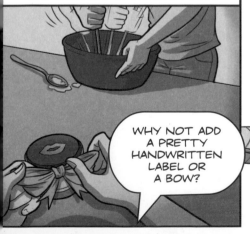

WHY NOT ADD A PRETTY HANDWRITTEN LABEL OR A BOW?

HOW TO HAVE THE BEST SLEEPOVER EVER

DO YOU WANT TO BE THE ENVY OF YOUR FRIENDS AND HOST THE BEST SLEEPOVER EVER? READ ON TO FIND OUT HOW.

GIVE YOUR SLEEPOVER A THEME. IT COULD BE ANYTHING, FROM 'PINK' TO 'SPOOKY'. DECORATE YOUR ROOM TO MAKE IT REALLY SPECIAL.

I'VE CHOSEN A HOLLYWOOD GLAMOUR THEME.

YOUR GUESTS CAN DRESS UP IN THE PERFECT OUTFITS.

PLAN LOTS OF THINGS TO DO AT YOUR SLEEPOVER. YOU COULD EXPERIMENT WITH NEW LOOKS ...

... OR PAMPER YOURSELVES.

YOU COULD MAKE A TASTY
SNACK TOGETHER ...

... OR TEST YOUR DANCING SKILLS.

DVDS ARE A SLEEPOVER STAPLE.
HAVE A SELECTION READY TO SUIT THE MOOD.

TRY A
ROMCOM ...

... OR A
WEEPY FILM ...

... OR A SCARY FILM, IF
YOU'RE FEELING BRAVE.

REMIND YOUR GUESTS TO
PACK WISELY.

AND TO BRING SUPPLIES FOR
THE MOST IMPORTANT PART
OF THE SLEEPOVER ...

... THE MIDNIGHT FEAST!

HOW TO LOOK YOUR BEST FOR A PARTY

DO YOU WANT TO LOOK YOUR VERY BEST FOR A PARTY?
FOLLOW OUR TIPS TO BE A TRULY GORGEOUS GIRL.

PREPARATIONS CAN **NEVER** BE RUSHED.

A GORGEOUS GIRL MAKES SURE HER SKIN IS SUPER-SOFT.

DON'T FORGET THAT SOME PLACES NEED A LITTLE EXTRA ATTENTION.

ENJOY GETTING READY. IF YOU'RE RELAXED, YOU'LL LOOK GREAT.

ALLOW PLENTY OF TIME FOR THOSE BIG DECISIONS.

A GORGEOUS GIRL KNOWS THE THREE RULES OF THE PERFECT BLOW DRY ...

1. FIRST ADD BODY TO THE ROOTS.

2. POINT THE DRYER DOWN THE LENGTH OF THE HAIR TO ADD SHINE.

3. A FINAL COOL BLAST FIXES THE STYLE.

... AND THE BEST WAY TO PAINT HER NAILS.

ALWAYS PAINT TWO COATS!

1. PAINT ONE STRIPE DOWN THE CENTRE.

2. ONE DOWN THE LEFT-HAND SIDE.

3. THEN ONE DOWN THE RIGHT-HAND SIDE.

ACCESSORIES WILL REALLY MAKE YOUR OUTFIT.

FINALLY, A GORGEOUS GIRL NEVER FORGETS TO PRACTISE THE MOST IMPORTANT THING OF ALL - A DAZZLING SMILE!

HOW TO SURVIVE SIBLINGS

BROTHERS ARE STRANGE THINGS.

THEY HAVE STRANGE HABITS ...

... AND EAT VERY STRANGE FOOD.

SO HERE'S HOW TO DEAL WITH THEM:

1. **NEVER** GO INTO YOUR BROTHER'S ROOM WITHOUT BEING FULLY PREPARED.

2. YOUR DIARY MUST BE PROTECTED AT ALL COSTS.

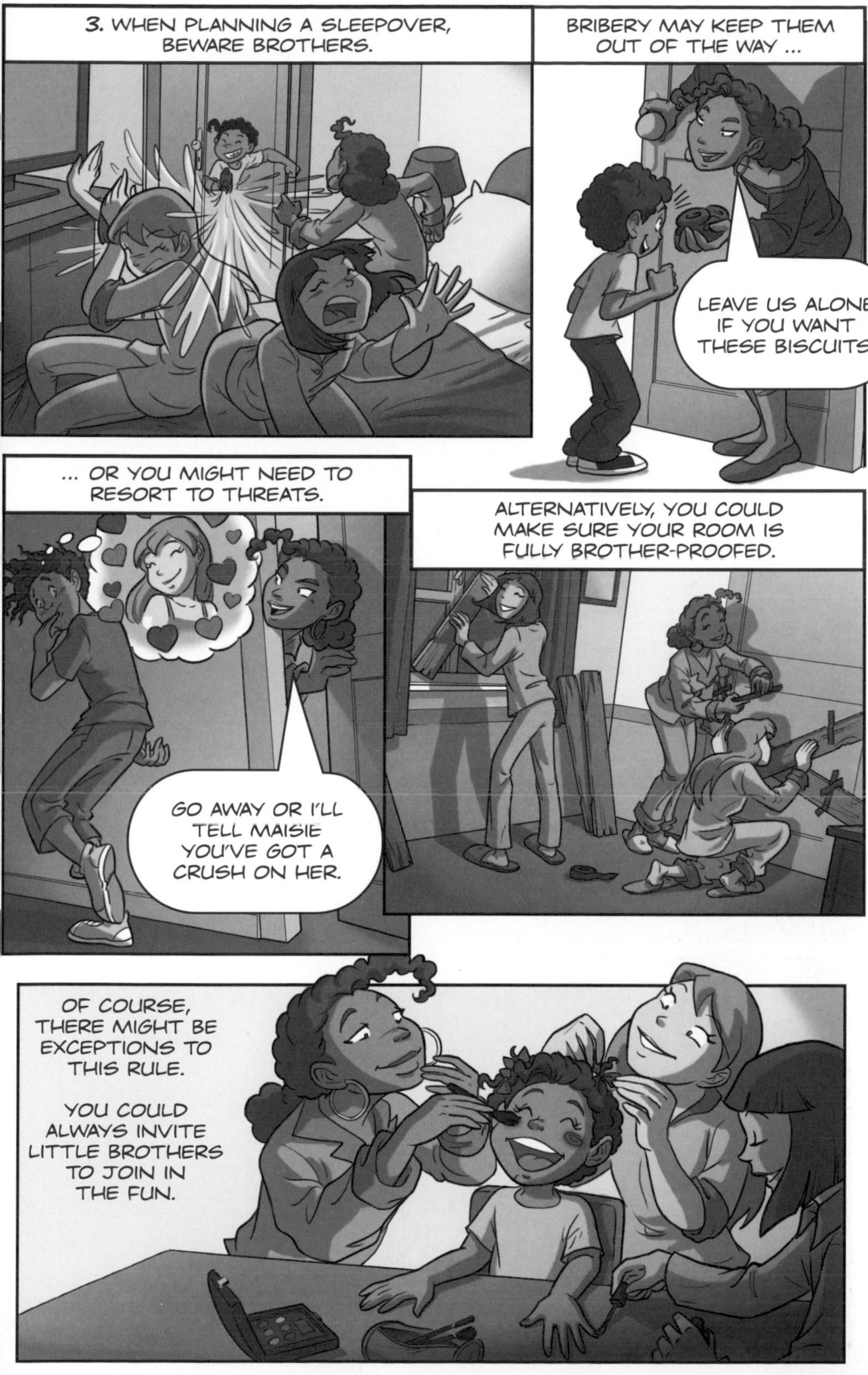
3. WHEN PLANNING A SLEEPOVER, BEWARE BROTHERS.
BRIBERY MAY KEEP THEM OUT OF THE WAY ...
LEAVE US ALONE IF YOU WANT THESE BISCUITS.
... OR YOU MIGHT NEED TO RESORT TO THREATS.
GO AWAY OR I'LL TELL MAISIE YOU'VE GOT A CRUSH ON HER.
ALTERNATIVELY, YOU COULD MAKE SURE YOUR ROOM IS FULLY BROTHER-PROOFED.
OF COURSE, THERE MIGHT BE EXCEPTIONS TO THIS RULE.
YOU COULD ALWAYS INVITE LITTLE BROTHERS TO JOIN IN THE FUN.

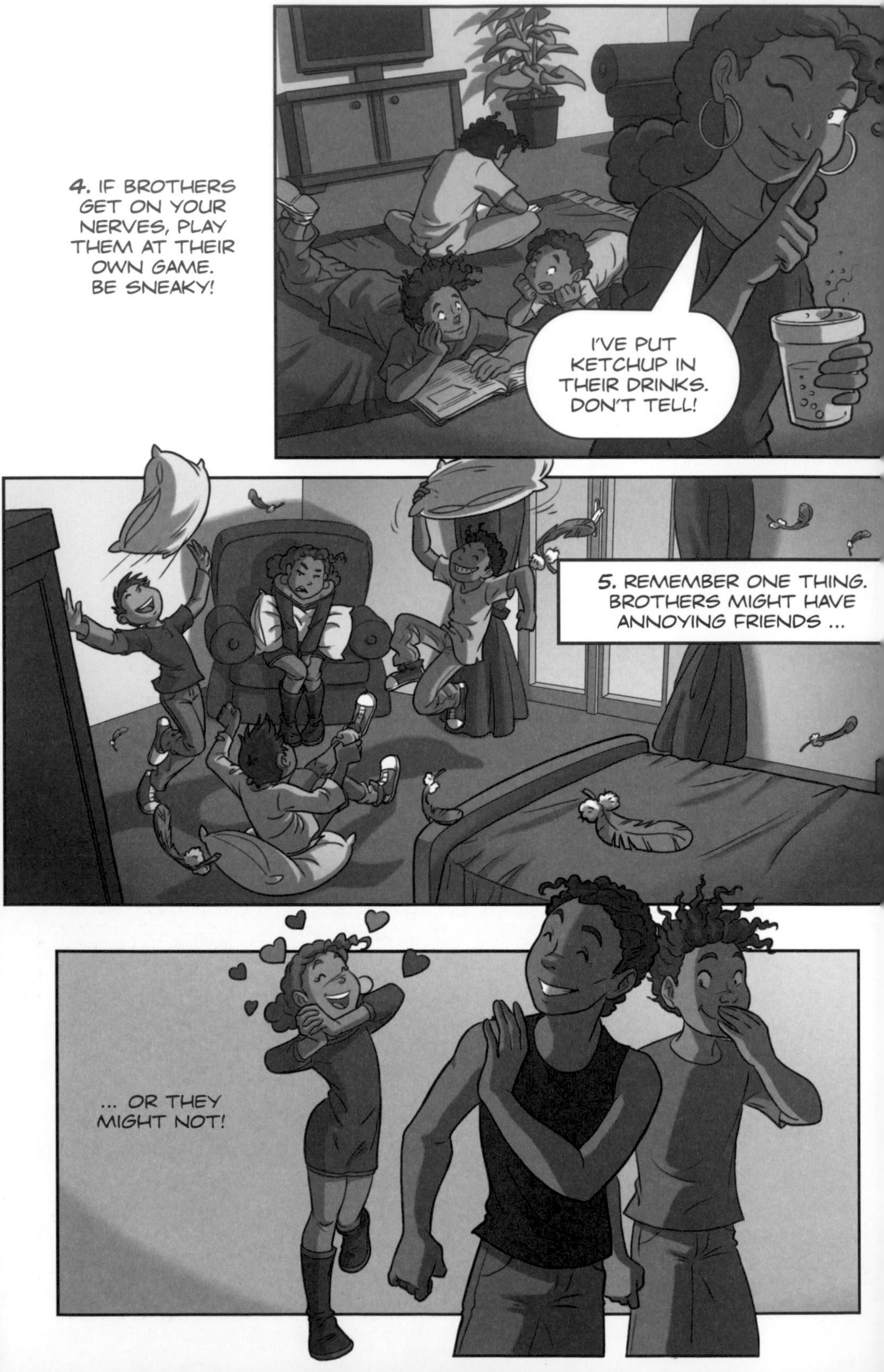
4. IF BROTHERS GET ON YOUR NERVES, PLAY THEM AT THEIR OWN GAME. BE SNEAKY!
I'VE PUT KETCHUP IN THEIR DRINKS. DON'T TELL!
5. REMEMBER ONE THING. BROTHERS MIGHT HAVE ANNOYING FRIENDS ...
... OR THEY MIGHT NOT!

SCARY SURVIVAL DOS AND DON'TS

FOLLOW THE DOS AND DON'TS BELOW IF YOU HAPPEN TO FIND YOURSELF IN A MONSTROUS SITUATION.

1. YOUR FRIEND APPEARS TO HAVE FANGS. **DO** INVENT AN EXCUSE TO GO HOME IMMEDIATELY.

IT MUST BE SOMETHING I ATE ...

DON'T ASK HIM TO ADMIRE YOUR EARRINGS.

2. YOU WAKE TO FIND A GHOST IN YOUR BEDROOM. **DO** LET YOUR GHOST CHAT. IT IS PROBABLY JUST BORED AND LONELY.

MUMMY NEVER UNDERSTOOD ME!

DON'T THROW THINGS OR SHOUT AT YOUR GHOST. IT MAY REACT BADLY.

3. AN ALIEN SPACESHIP LANDS IN THE PARK. **DO** SEIZE THIS CHANCE FOR A FRONT-PAGE SCOOP.

DON'T SNEEZE AT THE WRONG MOMENT. IF THE ALIENS NOTICE YOU, THEY MAY TAKE YOU BACK TO THEIR HOME PLANET.

ACHOO!

HOW TO HANDLE BECOMING RICH

IT'S GREAT NEWS WHEN YOU COME INTO SOME MONEY YOU'RE NOT EXPECTING. A SMALL WINDFALL CAN GIVE YOU SOME FUN DECISIONS TO MAKE.

SHOULD I SAVE IT?

OR SPEND IT?

BUT SUPPOSE YOUR ECCENTRIC GREAT UNCLE LEAVES YOU A HUGE FORTUNE. WHAT THEN?

HE LEFT ME ALL HIS MONEY? JUST ME?

WHEN YOU ARE RICH, YOU MAY FIND YOU BECOME A BIT OF A CELEBRITY. BE CAREFUL – INTERVIEWS CAN BE DAUNTING FOR THE COMPLETE BEGINNER ...

FIRST, DON'T CELEBRATE TO EXCESS.

OVERNIGHT, THE RICHEST GIRL IN THE WORLD!

... SO INVEST IN SOME MEDIA TRAINING.

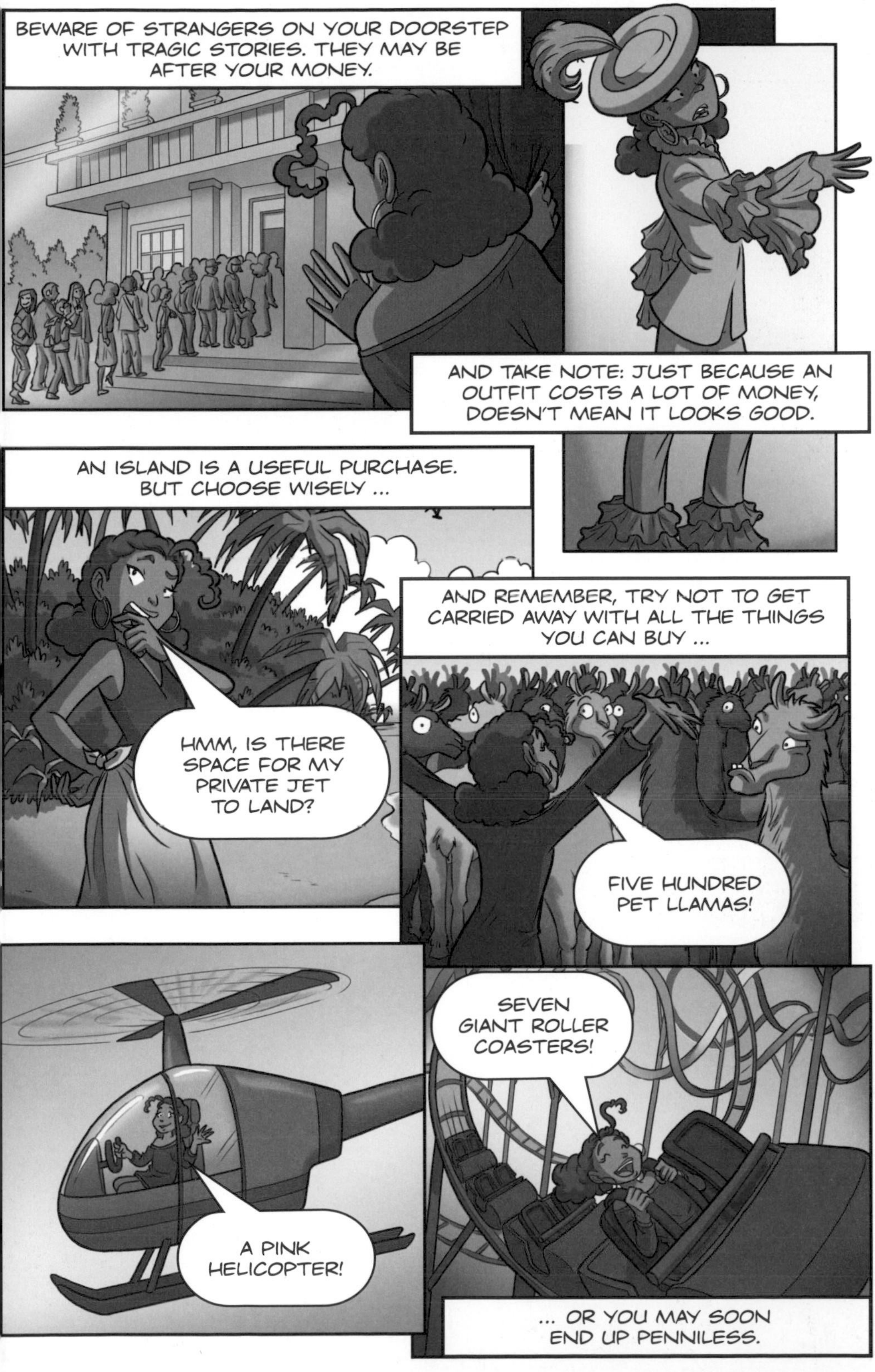
BEWARE OF STRANGERS ON YOUR DOORSTEP WITH TRAGIC STORIES. THEY MAY BE AFTER YOUR MONEY.
AND TAKE NOTE: JUST BECAUSE AN OUTFIT COSTS A LOT OF MONEY, DOESN'T MEAN IT LOOKS GOOD.
AN ISLAND IS A USEFUL PURCHASE. BUT CHOOSE WISELY ...
HMM, IS THERE SPACE FOR MY PRIVATE JET TO LAND?
AND REMEMBER, TRY NOT TO GET CARRIED AWAY WITH ALL THE THINGS YOU CAN BUY ...
FIVE HUNDRED PET LLAMAS!
A PINK HELICOPTER!
SEVEN GIANT ROLLER COASTERS!
... OR YOU MAY SOON END UP PENNILESS.

HOW TO KEEP STUFF SECRET

SOMETIMES GIRLS NEED TO PASS ON VITAL SECRET INFORMATION.

BEWARE! ENEMIES MAY BE LURKING AROUND EVERY CORNER ...

... READY TO STEAL YOUR SECRETS.

BUT EVERY SPY HAS A SECRET WEAPON – INVISIBLE INK.

THERE'S NOTHING HERE!

HERE'S HOW YOU MAKE IT.

MIX TOGETHER EQUAL AMOUNTS OF WATER AND BICARBONATE OF SODA. YOU ONLY NEED A LITTLE OF BOTH!

DIP A TOOTHPICK IN THE MIXTURE AND WRITE YOUR MESSAGE.

A COTTON BUD WORKS, TOO.

THEN PASS IT ON TO A GIRL IN THE KNOW WHO CAN REVEAL YOUR SECRET MESSAGE USING THE HEAT FROM A HAIRDRYER!

INVISIBLE INK ISN'T PRACTICAL IN EVERY SITUATION. SOMETIMES A SECRET CODE IS BEST.

HERE'S A SIMPLE ONE TO GET YOU STARTED. TRY USING SYMBOLS INSTEAD OF PHRASES.

AFTERNOON

CRUSH

TOMORROW

TO DISCUSS

MEET ME

SECRET

CAN YOU UNLOCK THE MESSAGE IN THE NOTE?

OF COURSE, SOMETIMES IT'S BETTER NOT TO WRITE ANYTHING DOWN AT ALL. WHY NOT USE HAND SIGNALS OR BODY MOVEMENTS TO CONVEY INFORMATION INSTANTLY?

SCRATCH!

YAWN!

MEANS: I'M BORED – LET'S LEAVE IMMEDIATELY.

MEANS: DON'T LOOK – HE'S BEHIND YOU.

MEANS: LET'S CHANGE LOCATION.

TUG

MEANS: SOMEONE'S LISTENING TO OUR CONVERSATION.

CROSS OVER

IT'S NEARLY TEST TIME, AND YOU NEED TO REVISE THIS TERM'S WORK.
DON'T PANIC, JUST FOLLOW THESE TIPS.

1. GIVE YOURSELF PLENTY OF TIME. IF YOU LEAVE ALL YOUR REVISION TO THE NIGHT BEFORE ...

... YOU MAY REGRET IT.

2. CHOOSE WHERE YOU REVISE CAREFULLY. A QUIET ROOM WITH A CLEAR DESK IS FAR BETTER THAN A ROOM WHERE THE TV IS BLARING AND THE DOG IS BARKING.

3. LOOK AT YOUR TEST TIMETABLE AND ASK YOURSELF SOME QUESTIONS, THEN PLAN YOUR REVISION AHEAD. IT HELPS IF YOU PLAN WHAT YOU NEED TO REVISE EACH DAY.

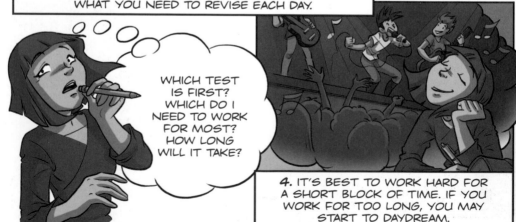

WHICH TEST IS FIRST? WHICH DO I NEED TO WORK FOR MOST? HOW LONG WILL IT TAKE?

4. IT'S BEST TO WORK HARD FOR A SHORT BLOCK OF TIME. IF YOU WORK FOR TOO LONG, YOU MAY START TO DAYDREAM.

5. WHEN YOU TAKE A BREAK, DO SOMETHING COMPLETELY DIFFERENT.

BUT DON'T LET YOURSELF GET DISTRACTED FOR TOO LONG.

6. THERE ARE LOTS OF DIFFERENT WAYS TO REVISE.

TIME TO DO A PRACTICE TEST.

I'LL ASK YOU QUESTIONS FIRST, THEN WE'LL SWAP OVER.

IT CAN HELP TO SWITCH FROM ONE SUBJECT TO ANOTHER, SO YOU DON'T GET BORED.

TIME FOR SOME MATHS NOW.

... OR KEEPING QUIET.

SHHH!

7. LET YOUR FAMILY KNOW WHEN YOU'RE WORKING, SO THEY CAN BE SUPPORTIVE, BY BRINGING DRINKS ...

8. REMEMBER, NOT EVERYONE IS TOP OF THE CLASS. JUST DO THE BEST YOU CAN, AND AFTER YOUR TESTS ARE OVER, HAVE FUN!

HOW TO SURVIVE SHYNESS

INVITATION FOR YOU!

HURRAH, YOU'VE GOT A PARTY INVITATION!

COME TO MY BIRTHDAY

BUT THE ONLY PERSON YOU'LL KNOW IS THE BIRTHDAY GIRL.

KEEP CALM. JUST SMILE AND ACT FRIENDLY, SO OTHER PEOPLE WILL WANT TO TALK TO YOU. THE KEY IS TO MAKE EYE CONTACT.

HI, I'M MILLIE.

NO ONE FINDS NEW FRIENDS ON THE FLOOR. DON'T STARE AT YOUR FEET – LOOK UP AND AROUND YOU.

AND REMEMBER, YOU PROBABLY WON'T BE THE ONLY SHY GIRL THERE.

HI!

HI!

IF YOU SEE SOMEONE ELSE ON THEIR OWN, BE BRAVE AND SAY HELLO.

A COMPLIMENT IS A GOOD WAY TO START A CONVERSATION.

I LIKE YOUR T-SHIRT.

ALTHOUGH TOO MANY MAY MAKE YOU SEEM A BIT STRANGE.

YOUR HAIR IS AMAZING.

I LOVE YOUR NAILS.

THOSE SHOES ARE SO COOL.

QUESTIONS ARE A GOOD WAY TO BREAK THE ICE. THERE ARE LOTS OF THINGS YOU COULD ASK ABOUT.

FAMILY? HOBBIES? FAVOURITE LESSON?

YOU **CAN** ASK A QUESTION SUCH AS ...

DO YOU LIKE WATCHING TV?

YES.

... BUT QUESTIONS THAT START WITH 'WHAT', 'WHERE', 'WHICH' OR 'WHO' ARE EVEN BETTER, BECAUSE THEY NEED MORE THAN A ONE-WORD ANSWER.

WHAT'S YOUR FAVOURITE TV SHOW?

BEFORE YOU KNOW IT, YOU'LL BE CHATTING AWAY.

HA HA!

HA HA!

HOW TO HANDLE SUDDEN STARDOM

DO YOU FEEL LIKE YOU'RE ON THE BRINK OF BECOMING FAMOUS?
HERE ARE A FEW TIPS ON HOW TO HANDLE SUDDEN STARDOM.

INVENT A DAZZLING AUTOGRAPH. SHORTEN YOUR
NAME – SHOWBIZ-STYLE – AND ADD SOME SWIRLS.

BUT BEWARE, YOU MAY
BE ASKED TO SIGN
SOME STRANGE
THINGS.

IF YOUR WRIST GETS TIRED FROM SIGNING ...

... STRAP IT UP AND
ADD SOME BLING!

LOOK LIKE A
STAR WITH ALL
THE RIGHT
ACCESSORIES,
INCLUDING A
PERFECT POOCH.

REMEMBER, THE PAPARAZZI ARE EVERYWHERE.

SO WATCH YOUR STEP OR *YOU* COULD BE FRONT-PAGE NEWS!

IT'S NEVER TOO SOON TO PREPARE YOUR OSCARS SPEECH ...

THIS AWARD ISN'T JUST FOR ME ...

... OR TO PRACTISE YOUR RED CARPET POSES.

BUT MOST IMPORTANTLY, REMEMBER TO BE HUMBLE AND GRACIOUS AT ALL TIMES. TURN THE PAGE FOR WHAT *NOT* TO DO IF YOU BECOME A STAR.

MORE STARDOM SURVIVAL TIPS

WE'VE TOLD YOU WHAT TO DO WHEN STARDOM STRIKES,
BUT DON'T BE A DIVA – HERE'S WHAT **NOT** TO DO!

I ASKED FOR PINK SLIPPERS WITH POMPOMS. HOW DARE YOU BRING ME THESE?

I SAID SIX HEART-SHAPED ICE CUBES!

SCHOOLWORK IS NOT FOR SUPERSTARS!

I ONLY EVER EAT BROCCOLI WHEN IT'S A FULL MOON!

REMEMBER, DIVA-LIKE BEHAVIOUR MIGHT GET YOU INTO THE PAGES OF A GOSSIP MAGAZINE, BUT IT WILL BE FOR ALL THE **WRONG** REASONS.

HOW TO SURVIVE A CAMPING TRIP

CAMPING MAY NOT ALWAYS BE A GIRL'S TOP CHOICE OF ACTIVITY.

BUT HERE'S HOW TO MAKE THE BEST OF A BAD SITUATION, AND SURVIVE IN STYLE.

CAMPING IS AN OUTDOOR ACTIVITY – SO PACK CAREFULLY, FOR **ALL** WEATHERS.

BE POSITIVE! REMEMBER, BAD WEATHER CAN'T LAST FOREVER.

WOW, WHAT A STUNNING VIEW!

BESIDES, FRESH AIR IS EXCELLENT FOR THE SKIN. AND A BRISK WALK IS A MARVELLOUS WORKOUT.

THE NIGHTS CAN GET EXTRA CHILLY, SO BRING WARM LAYERS ...

... AND A TORCH.

WHOOPS!

BUT DON'T FORGET, NIGHT-TIME CAN ALSO BE THE BEST PART OF THE TRIP!

HOW TO SURVIVE A FASHION DISASTER

IT'S PARTY TIME – AND YOU HAVE **NOTHING** TO WEAR.

MUM'S NO HELP.

YOU'VE GOT LOTS OF CLOTHES!

NOR IS YOUR BROTHER.

NO LOANS!

AND DON'T EVEN BOTHER ASKING YOUR SISTER.

NO, NO, NO.

IT'S TIME TO GET CREATIVE!

SOME FABRIC GLUE AND A FEW SEQUINS OR BEADS CAN TURN THIS ...

... INTO THIS.

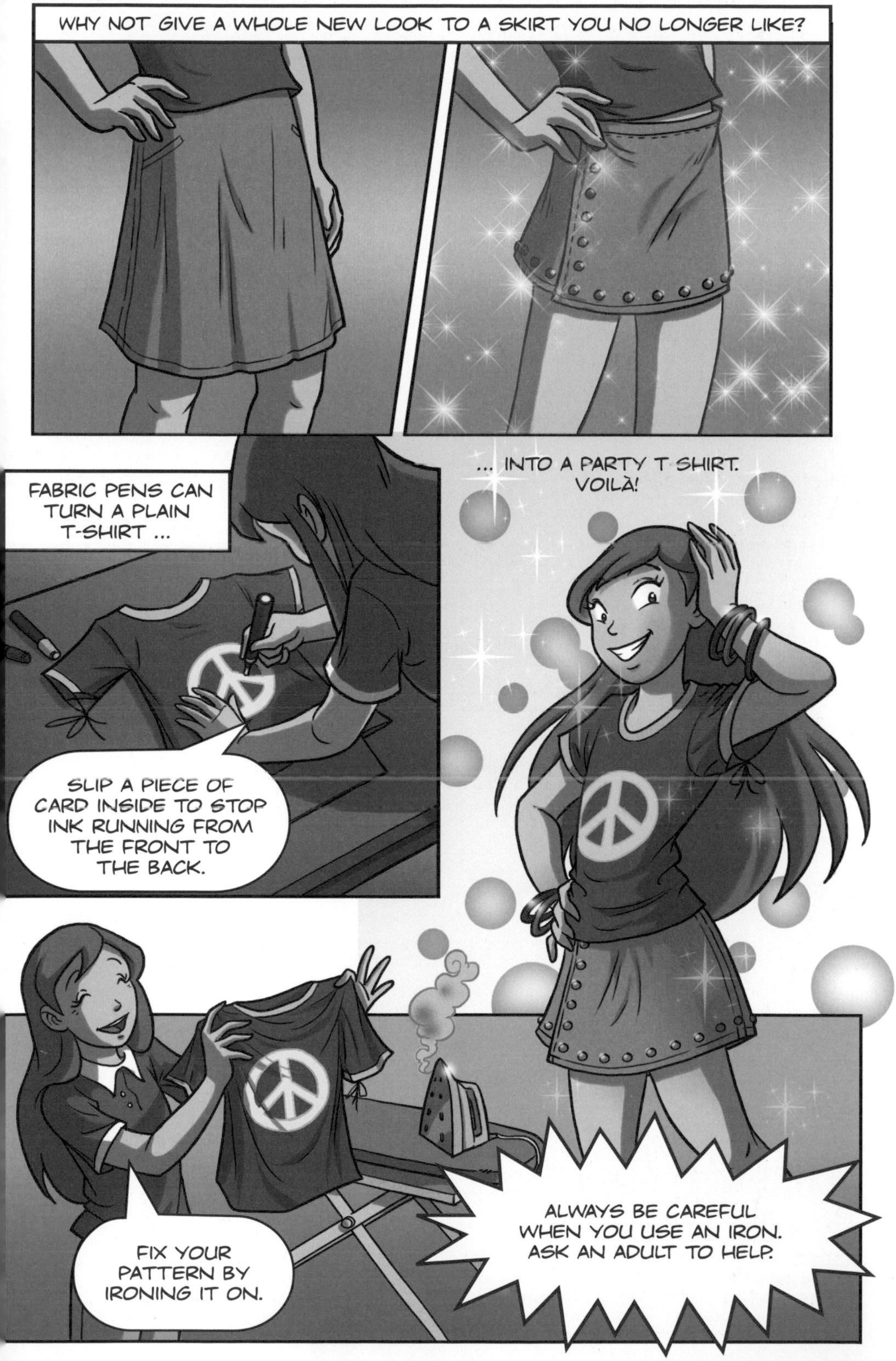
WHY NOT GIVE A WHOLE NEW LOOK TO A SKIRT YOU NO LONGER LIKE?
FABRIC PENS CAN TURN A PLAIN T-SHIRT ...
SLIP A PIECE OF CARD INSIDE TO STOP INK RUNNING FROM THE FRONT TO THE BACK.
... INTO A PARTY T SHIRT. VOILÀ!
FIX YOUR PATTERN BY IRONING IT ON.
ALWAYS BE CAREFUL WHEN YOU USE AN IRON. ASK AN ADULT TO HELP.

HAVE YOU ALWAYS WANTED A DOG, BUT BEEN UNABLE TO PERSUADE YOUR PARENTS? NEVER FEAR – TRY TEACHING YOUR CAT THIS TRICK INSTEAD.

MANY PEOPLE THINK THAT OUR FELINE FRIENDS ARE JUST TOO INDEPENDENT TO BE TAUGHT TRICKS.

BUT THAT'S NOT TRUE. YOU REALLY *CAN* TEACH YOUR CAT TO SIT. HERE'S HOW.

1. BEFORE YOU START, MAKE SURE YOUR CAT IS FEELING RELAXED, SO THAT IT WILL BE MORE WILLING TO LEARN.

2. SHOW YOUR CAT AN EDIBLE TREAT, SUCH AS A CAT BISCUIT, AND SAY, 'FLUFFY – INSERT YOUR CAT'S NAME HERE – SIT.'

3. MOVE THE TREAT BACKWARDS OVER YOUR CAT'S HEAD. AS IT WATCHES THE TREAT, IT SHOULD SIT DOWN TO BALANCE.

IF IT DOESN'T, GENTLY PRESS DOWN ON ITS HINDQUARTERS. DON'T PUSH TOO HARD, OR YOUR CAT MIGHT GET ANGRY.

4. AS YOUR CAT SITS, GIVE IT LOTS OF PRAISE, AND, OF COURSE, A TREAT – OR MORE IF YOU FEEL LIKE IT.

TOP TIP: YOU MIGHT GET BETTER RESULTS IF YOU TRAIN YOUR CAT WHEN IT'S HUNGRY.

IF YOU FIND THAT EITHER YOU OR THE CAT IS BECOMING FRUSTRATED, LEAVE IT UNTIL ANOTHER TIME.

BE PATIENT, AND KEEP PRACTISING.

ONCE YOUR CAT LEARNS THAT WHEN IT SITS IT GETS A TREAT, IT'LL DO IT AUTOMATICALLY. AND THAT'S HOW YOU CAN TEACH YOUR CAT TO SIT.

HOW TO TURN A NO INTO A YES

SOME GROWN-UPS ARE NOT KEEN ON CATS – OR ANY PETS.

NO WAY.

HOWEVER, HERE ARE SOME WAYS TO CHANGE A GROWN-UP'S MIND.

1. BE REASONABLE. OFFER YOUR GROWN-UP A VARIETY OF OPTIONS.

NO.

2. THINK OF THE REASONS WHY THE ANSWER IS NO, AND TRY TO WORK AROUND THEM.

IF SPACE IS A PROBLEM, THINK SMALL.

THE ANSWER IS STILL NO.

3. PROMISE YOUR GROWN-UP YOU WILL LOOK AFTER YOUR PET.

HERE'S A SIGNED CONTRACT.

NO.

4. DO SOME CHORES TO EARN MONEY ...

... THEN OFFER TO HELP WITH THE COSTS OF YOUR PET.

NO!

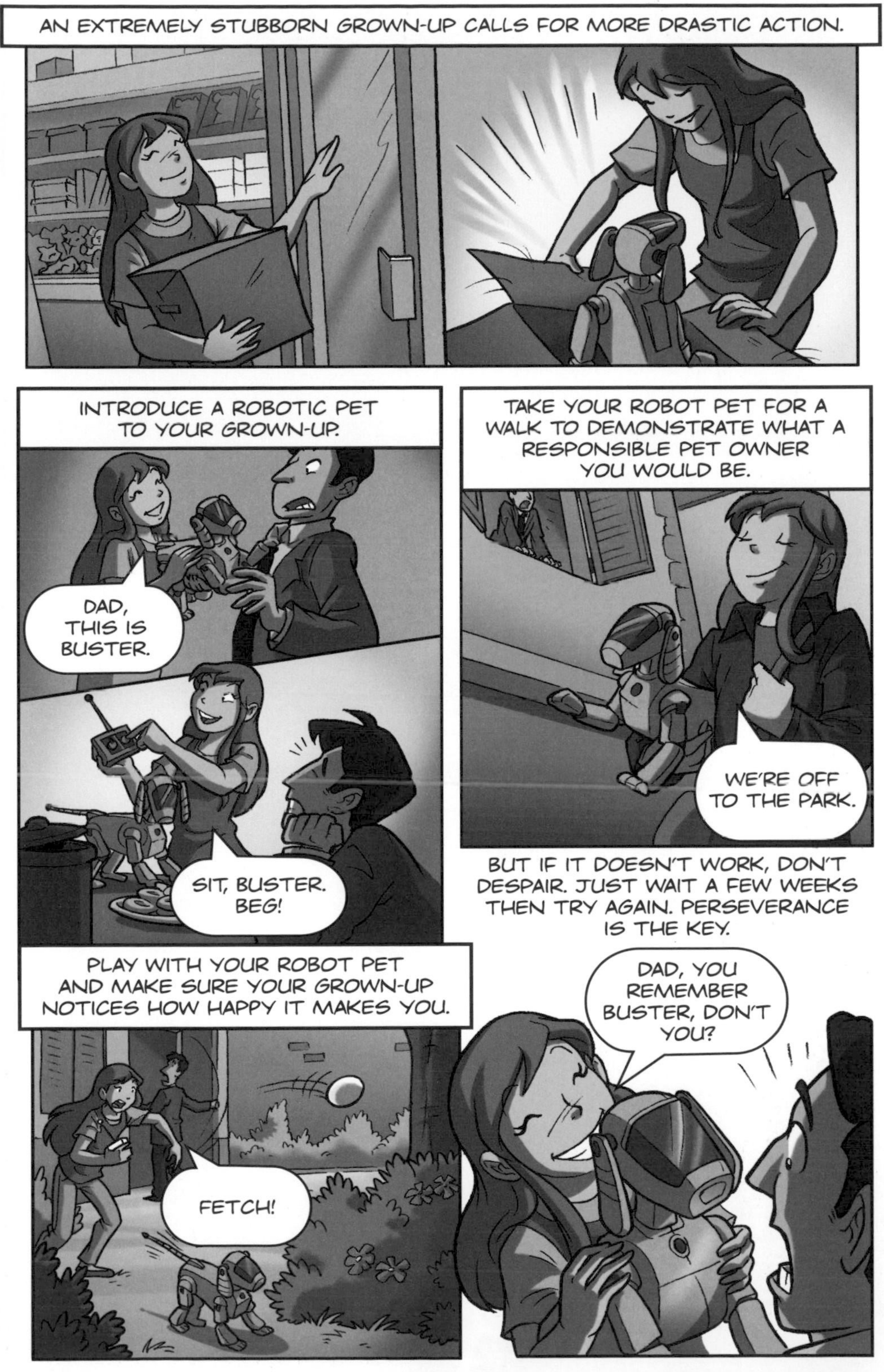

AN EXTREMELY STUBBORN GROWN-UP CALLS FOR MORE DRASTIC ACTION.
INTRODUCE A ROBOTIC PET TO YOUR GROWN-UP.
DAD, THIS IS BUSTER.
SIT, BUSTER. BEG!
PLAY WITH YOUR ROBOT PET AND MAKE SURE YOUR GROWN-UP NOTICES HOW HAPPY IT MAKES YOU.
FETCH!
TAKE YOUR ROBOT PET FOR A WALK TO DEMONSTRATE WHAT A RESPONSIBLE PET OWNER YOU WOULD BE.
WE'RE OFF TO THE PARK.
BUT IF IT DOESN'T WORK, DON'T DESPAIR. JUST WAIT A FEW WEEKS THEN TRY AGAIN. PERSEVERANCE IS THE KEY.
DAD, YOU REMEMBER BUSTER, DON'T YOU?

TOP TIPS FOR SPEECH-MAKING

YOU'VE BEEN ASKED TO MAKE A SPEECH AT SCHOOL. DON'T BE TERRIFIED OF SPEAKING IN PUBLIC, IT'S EASY IF YOU KNOW HOW. JUST FOLLOW THESE TIPS TO BECOME A TRULY STYLISH PUBLIC SPEAKER.

TO MAKE THE BEST SPEECH YOU CAN, PLAN IN ADVANCE. ALLOW LOTS OF TIME TO PREPARE.

LEARN YOUR SPEECH BY HEART ...

... BECAUSE READING IT FROM A PIECE OF PAPER WITHOUT LOOKING UP IS VERY BORING ...

... AND MAY CAUSE INJURY TO MEMBERS OF THE AUDIENCE.

A STYLISH SPEECH-MAKER KEEPS HER COOL BY FOCUSING ON A FRIEND.

BUT DON'T STARE AT ONE PERSON FOR TOO LONG. EVERYONE IN THE AUDIENCE SHOULD FEEL INCLUDED.

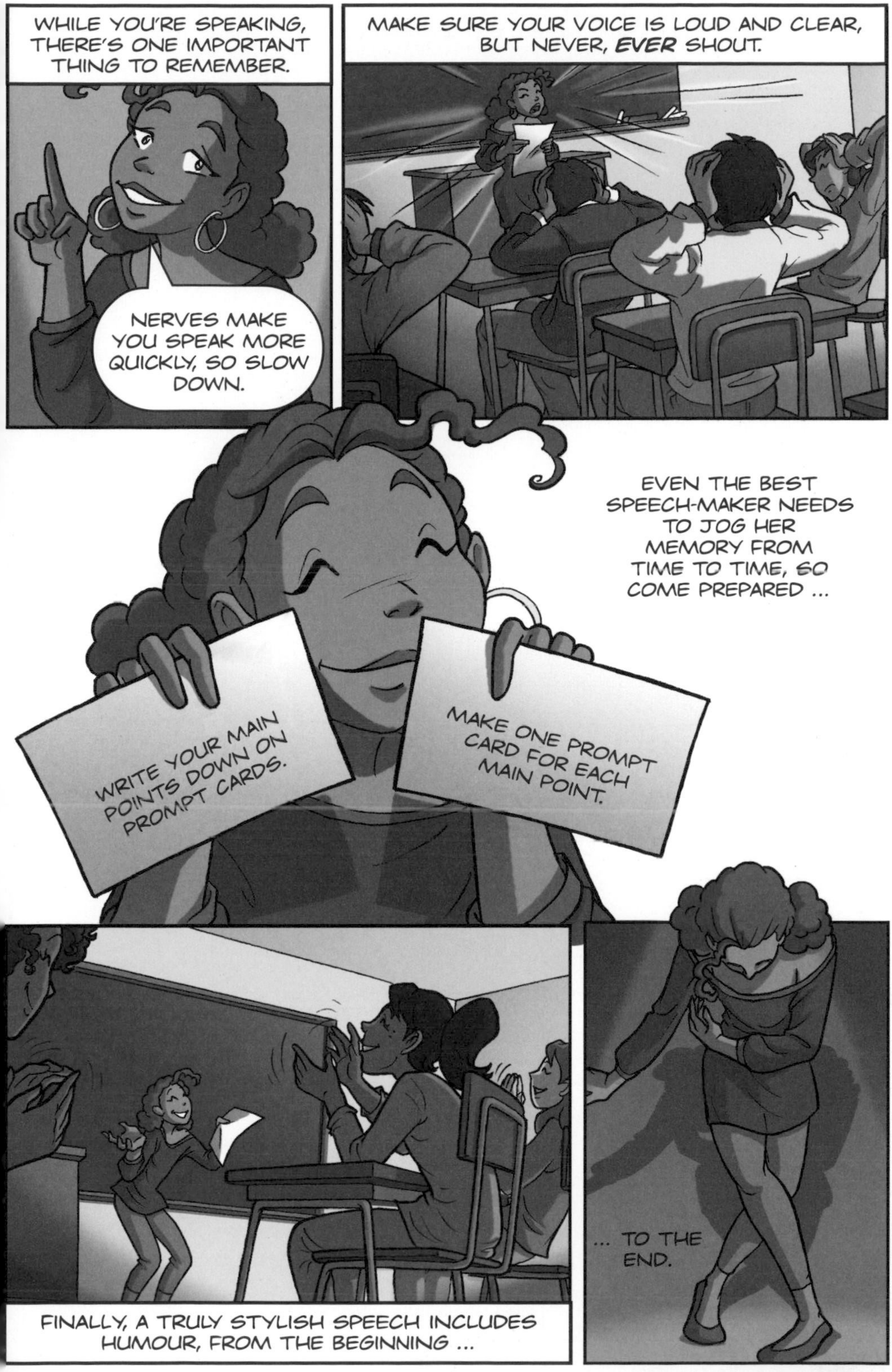
WHILE YOU'RE SPEAKING, THERE'S ONE IMPORTANT THING TO REMEMBER.
NERVES MAKE YOU SPEAK MORE QUICKLY, SO SLOW DOWN.
MAKE SURE YOUR VOICE IS LOUD AND CLEAR, BUT NEVER, ***EVER*** SHOUT.
EVEN THE BEST SPEECH-MAKER NEEDS TO JOG HER MEMORY FROM TIME TO TIME, SO COME PREPARED ...
WRITE YOUR MAIN POINTS DOWN ON PROMPT CARDS.
MAKE ONE PROMPT CARD FOR EACH MAIN POINT.
FINALLY, A TRULY STYLISH SPEECH INCLUDES HUMOUR, FROM THE BEGINNING ...
... TO THE END.

HOW TO SURVIVE EMBARRASSMENT

AN EMBARRASSING MOMENT CAN HAPPEN WHEN YOU LEAST EXPECT IT, SUCH AS TURNING UP TO A PARTY IN THE SAME DRESS AS A FRIEND.

THE TRICK IS HOW YOU GET OUT OF IT! DON'T HIDE AWAY ...

... OR TRY TO COVER UP.

WHY NOT DO THIS INSTEAD?

HEY, GOOD CHOICE OF OUTFIT!

WHEN EMBARRASSMENT STRIKES, BE COOL, CALM AND COLLECTED. HOLD YOUR HEAD UP HIGH AND STYLE IT OUT!

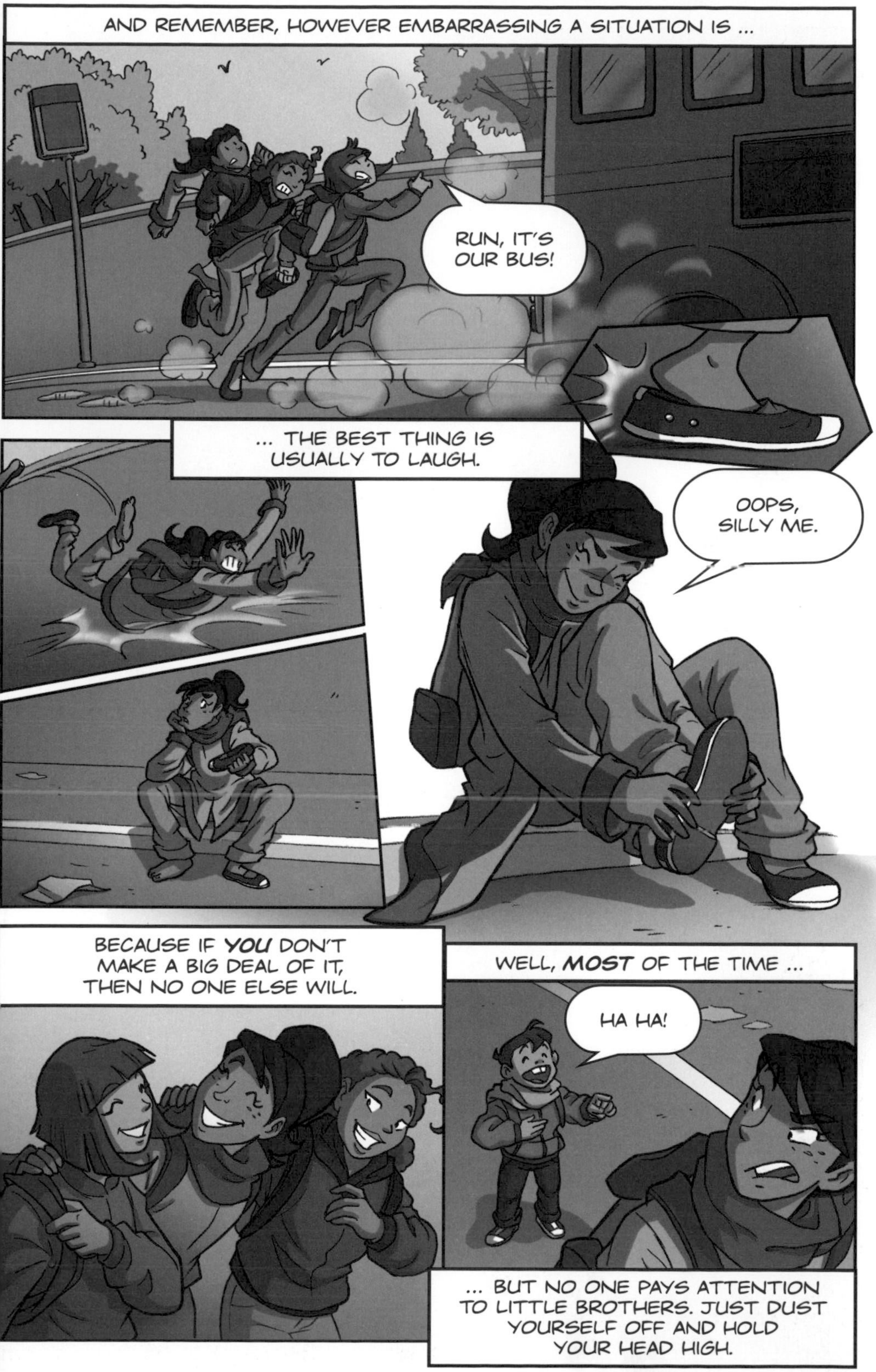
AND REMEMBER, HOWEVER EMBARRASSING A SITUATION IS ...
RUN, IT'S OUR BUS!
... THE BEST THING IS USUALLY TO LAUGH.
OOPS, SILLY ME.
BECAUSE IF ***YOU*** DON'T MAKE A BIG DEAL OF IT, THEN NO ONE ELSE WILL.
WELL, ***MOST*** OF THE TIME ...
HA HA!
... BUT NO ONE PAYS ATTENTION TO LITTLE BROTHERS. JUST DUST YOURSELF OFF AND HOLD YOUR HEAD HIGH.

SOMETIMES YOU MAY NEED TO CREATE A DIVERSION TO HELP A FRIEND OUT OF AN EMBARRASSING SPOT.

DON'T TELL MISS JONES, BUT I HAVEN'T DONE MY HOMEWORK.

ACT FAST. GATHER EVERYONE AROUND YOU.

COME OVER HERE, EVERYONE.

IF THERE'S A HAT HANDY, GRAB IT. YOU'LL NEED IT IN A MINUTE.

IF NOT, IMPROVISE, YOU NEED A CONTAINER THAT WILL HOLD SMALL PIECES OF PAPER.

ASK EVERYONE IN YOUR AUDIENCE TO THINK OF A FAMOUS PERSON.

ASK EACH PERSON TO TELL YOU THE NAME THEY'VE THOUGHT OF. WRITE EACH NAME DOWN ON A PIECE OF PAPER, FOLD IT TWICE, AND PUT IT IN THE HAT.

DON'T LET ANYONE SEE WHAT YOU'RE WRITING.

GET SOMEONE TO PICK A PIECE OF PAPER OUT OF THE HAT, BUT DON'T LET THEM OPEN IT.

NOW FOR A BIT OF ACTING ...

OOH, WHAT IS IT? IT'S COMING TO ME ...

WRITE DOWN OR TELL THEM THE NAME OF THE FAMOUS PERSON YOU THINK THEY PICKED OUT OF THE HAT – AND AMAZE THEM.

IS THIS THE NAME?

IT IS!

HERE'S THE SECRET.

YOU WRITE THE SAME NAME ON EVERY PIECE OF PAPER!

WARNING: ONLY TRY THIS ONCE – AND GET RID OF THE EVIDENCE FAST.

HOW TO SURVIVE A CRUSH

YOU'VE HAD A CRUSH ON A BOY FOR WEEKS AND WEEKS AND **WEEKS**, AND TODAY HE'S WALKING STRAIGHT TOWARDS YOU. WHAT DO YOU DO?

1. KEEP CALM. REMEMBER, HE'S A PERSON, NOT A GOD.

2. IF HE ASKS YOU A QUESTION, TRY TO ANSWER IT ...

... SENSIBLY.

WHAT'S YOUR FAVOURITE FOOD?

CHOC ... ER ... CHOC ... PIZZA.

CHOCOLATE PIZZA?

3. YOUR CRUSH WILL APPRECIATE YOU DOING **SOME** OF THE TALKING ...

... BUT NOT ALL OF IT.

46

4. DON'T STRETCH THE TRUTH TO APPEAR INTERESTING ...

TENNIS IS MY FAVOURITE SPORT, TOO.

... BECAUSE YOU'LL PROBABLY GET FOUND OUT.

5. EATING MESSY FOOD IN FRONT OF YOUR CRUSH CAN BE TRICKY, SO CHOOSE WISELY.

6. REMEMBER, IT'S GOOD TO GAZE INTO YOUR CRUSH'S EYES ...

... BUT LOOK WHERE YOU'RE GOING.

GOOD LUCK!

SEASIDE SURVIVAL

EVERY GIRL WANTS TO BE A BEACH BEAUTY. HERE ARE
SEVEN IMPORTANT TIPS TO HELP YOU BECOME A SEASIDE SENSATION.

*1. WHEN ON THE BEACH, LESS IS MORE – THE CASUAL LOOK IS **DEFINITELY** THE BEST.*

2. CHOOSE COMFORTABLE, WELL-FITTING SWIM WEAR. IF IT'S TOO TIGHT, YOU'LL SPEND YOUR TIME FIDGETING. TOO LOOSE, AND YOU MIGHT LOSE IT IF YOU ENCOUNTER ANY BIG WAVES.

OUCH!

3. WATCH OUT FOR WIND. BEACHES CAN BE GUSTY PLACES.

IT'S BEST TO TIE YOUR HAIR BACK, AND BE CAREFUL WHAT YOU WEAR.

4. A BEACH BEAUTY ALWAYS PROTECTS HER SKIN FROM SUN DAMAGE.

5. FEELING HOT? RETREAT TO THE SHADE BETWEEN 11 AM AND 3 PM.

IF YOU STAY IN THE SUN, COVER UP.

6. IT'S THE FINISHING TOUCHES THAT'LL TURN YOU INTO A BEACH BEAUTY.

7. ADD A LARGE PAIR OF SUNGLASSES FOR A FINAL TOUCH OF GLAMOUR.

WHO KNOWS? THEY MAY COME IN HANDY ...

... FOR SOME SUBTLE HUNK-SPOTTING.

HOW TO SOOTHE SUNBURN

IF YOUR SKIN IS SORE AND SUNBURNT, IT'S TIME TO CALL IN THE RESCUE-REMEDY TEAM.

HALF A CUP OF WARM WATER

HALF A CUP OF OATS

HONEY

PLAIN YOGURT

A MIXING BOWL

A TABLESPOON

LET THE OATS SOAK IN THE WATER FOR A FEW MINUTES.

THEN MIX IN TWO TABLESPOONS EACH OF HONEY AND YOGURT.

YOUR RESCUE REMEDY IS READY! JUST AVOID PUTTING IT ROUND YOUR EYES.

RELAX FOR 15 MINUTES, THEN RINSE IT OFF WITH WARM WATER.

RESULT!

DON'T FORGET THAT IT'S SAFEST NOT TO GET SUNBURNT IN THE FIRST PLACE, SO ALWAYS WEAR SUN CREAM.

HOW TO PICK PERFECT SUNGLASSES

NO SUPERSTAR LEAVES THE HOUSE WITHOUT THE PERFECT PAIR OF SUNNIES. HERE'S HOW TO CHOOSE THE RIGHT ONES FOR THE SHAPE OF YOUR FACE.

FIRST, TAKE A GOOD LOOK AT YOUR FACE SHAPE IN THE MIRROR.

DRAW ROUND THE OUTLINE WITH LIPSTICK.

DON'T FORGET TO CLEAN IT OFF AFTERWARDS.

PICK THE FACE SHAPE THAT MOST RESEMBLES YOURS, TO FIND OUT WHAT SHAPE GLASSES WILL SUIT YOU.

ROUND: TRY BROAD SUNNIES, AS WIDE AS YOUR FACE. SQUARE FRAMES LOOK GOOD, TOO.

HEART-SHAPED: YOU NEED DELICATE GLASSES. FRAMELESS ONES WOULD ALSO LOOK GOOD.

SQUARE: YOUR FACE SUITS SOFT, GENTLY CURVED SHAPES AND OVALS.

OVAL: YOU'RE LUCKY! EVERY SHAPE SUITS YOU.

IF ZOMBIES ATTACK, IT'S IMPORTANT TO ACT QUICKLY, BECAUSE JUST ONE BITE FROM A ZOMBIE COULD TURN YOU INTO ONE, TOO.

SPOTTING AN APPROACHING ZOMBIE SHOULD BE EASY.

A LOLLING HEAD

A VACANT STARE

OUTSTRETCHED ARMS

A SLOW, STUMBLING WALK

DESPITE THE FACT THEY'RE DEAD, IT'S NOT AS EASY AS IT LOOKS TO KILL A ZOMBIE. READ ON TO DISCOVER HOW TO SURVIVE A ZOMBIE ENCOUNTER.

DO NOT WASTE YOUR TIME WITH THE FOLLOWING:

SIT.

THEY CANNOT BE TRAINED ...

YOU WILL NOT BITE.

... OR HYPNOTIZED.

BUT DON'T DESPAIR. YOU HAVE ONE BIG ADVANTAGE OVER A ZOMBIE – A BRAIN!

SO IF A ZOMBIE CORNERS YOU, OUTWIT IT. PRETEND TO BE A ZOMBIE, TOO. IF YOU CAN DRIBBLE, EVEN BETTER.

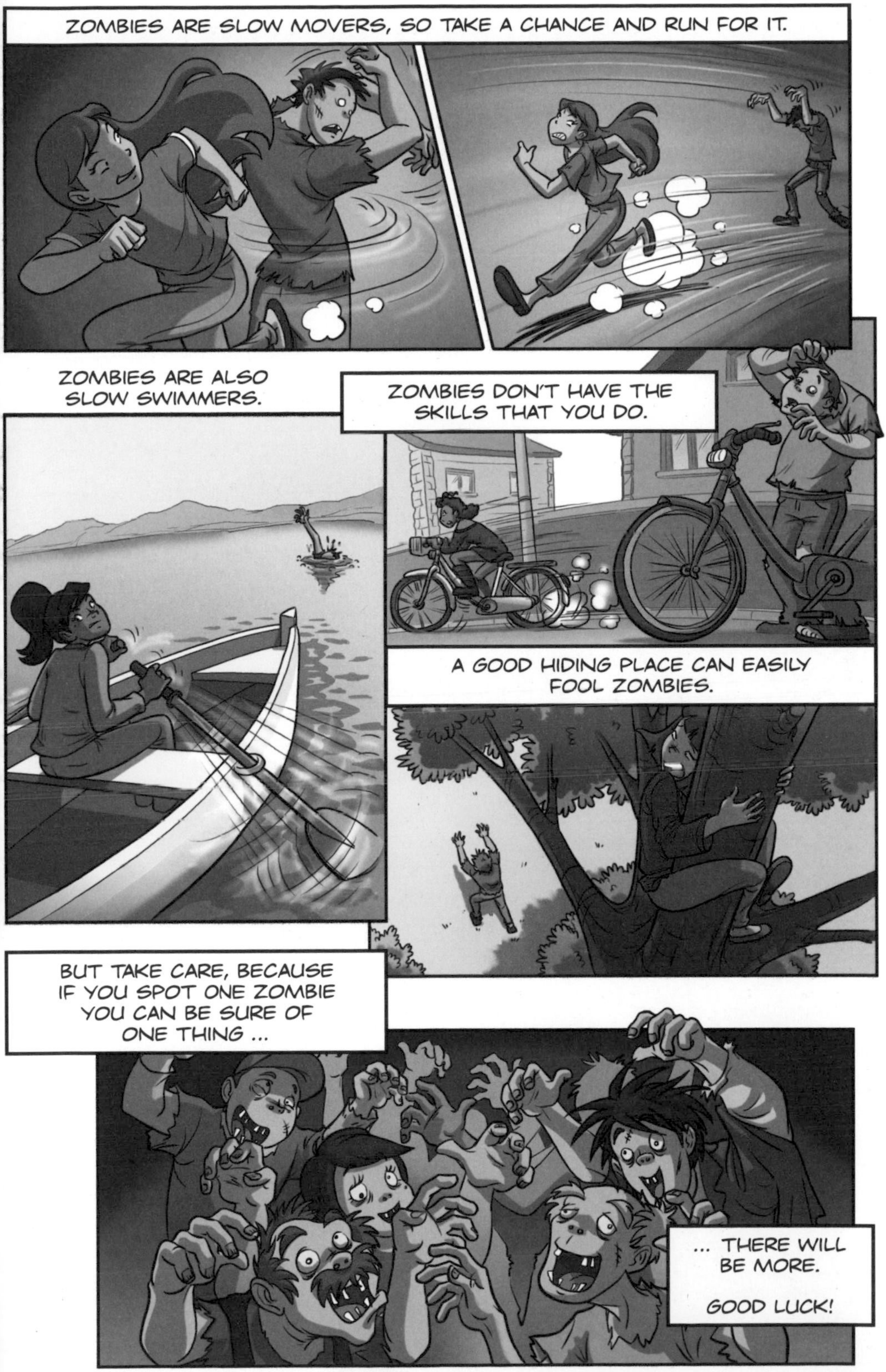
ZOMBIES ARE SLOW MOVERS, SO TAKE A CHANCE AND RUN FOR IT.
ZOMBIES ARE ALSO SLOW SWIMMERS.
ZOMBIES DON'T HAVE THE SKILLS THAT YOU DO.
A GOOD HIDING PLACE CAN EASILY FOOL ZOMBIES.
BUT TAKE CARE, BECAUSE IF YOU SPOT ONE ZOMBIE YOU CAN BE SURE OF ONE THING ...
... THERE WILL BE MORE.
GOOD LUCK!

HOW TO SPOT A FRENEMY

IT'S EASY TO RECOGNIZE YOUR TRUE FRIENDS. BUT 'FRENEMIES' ARE OFTEN HARDER TO SPOT. HERE'S WHAT TO LOOK OUT FOR.

A FRENEMY MAKES YOU FEEL BAD MOST OF THE TIME.

SHE MIGHT MAKE JOKES AT YOUR EXPENSE ...

SHE'S SO SHORT SHE'D FIT IN MY POCKET!

... OR NASTY COMMENTS.

WHY ARE YOU WEARING THAT? IT'S DISGUSTING!

SHE MIGHT MAKE YOU FEEL STUPID.

YOU MUST BE THE CLUMSIEST GIRL IN SCHOOL.

A FRENEMY DOESN'T SEEM TO CARE MUCH ABOUT YOU.

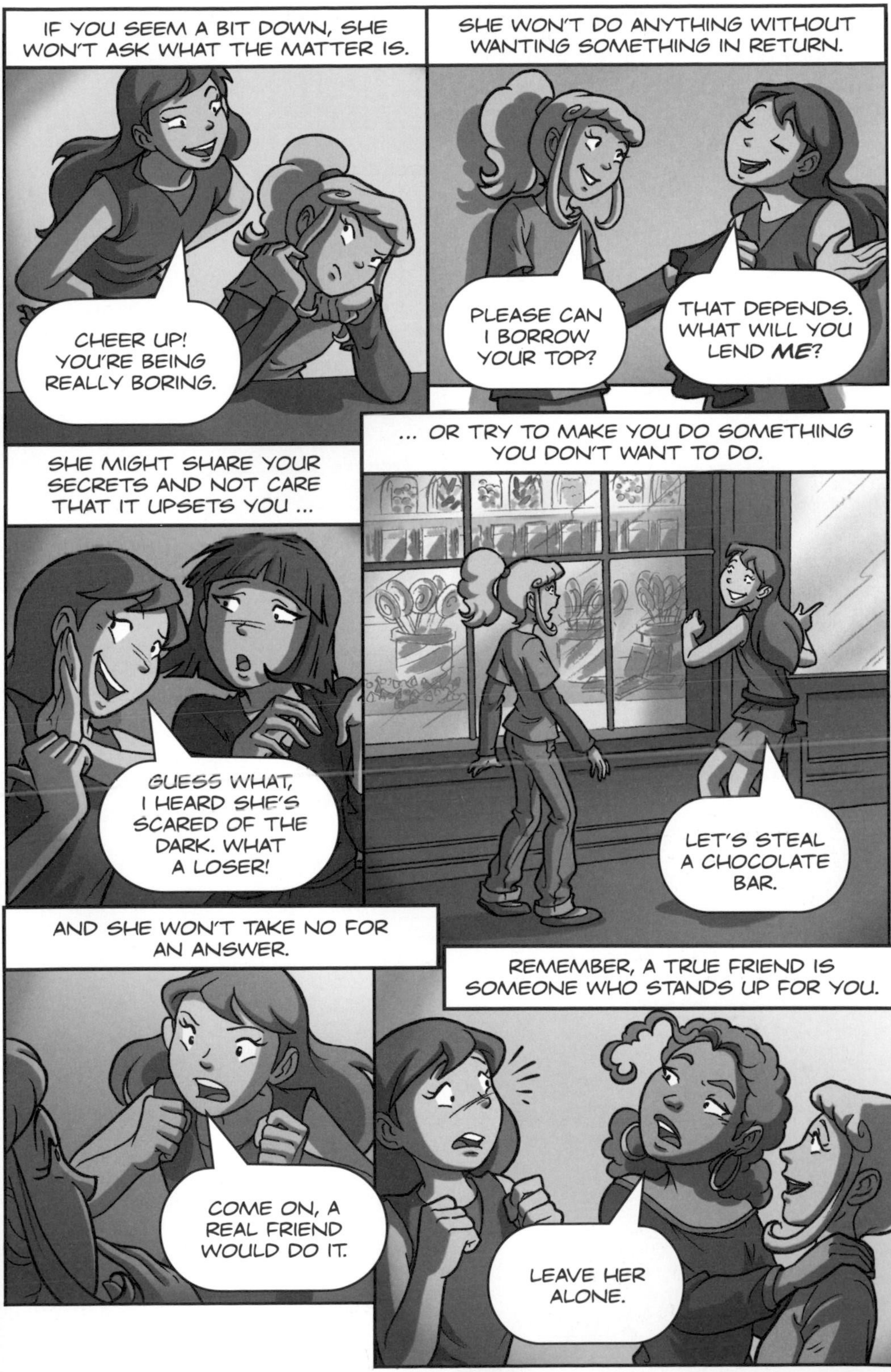

IF YOU SEEM A BIT DOWN, SHE WON'T ASK WHAT THE MATTER IS.
CHEER UP! YOU'RE BEING REALLY BORING.
SHE WON'T DO ANYTHING WITHOUT WANTING SOMETHING IN RETURN.
PLEASE CAN I BORROW YOUR TOP?
THAT DEPENDS. WHAT WILL YOU LEND *ME*?
SHE MIGHT SHARE YOUR SECRETS AND NOT CARE THAT IT UPSETS YOU ...
GUESS WHAT, I HEARD SHE'S SCARED OF THE DARK. WHAT A LOSER!
... OR TRY TO MAKE YOU DO SOMETHING YOU DON'T WANT TO DO.
LET'S STEAL A CHOCOLATE BAR.
AND SHE WON'T TAKE NO FOR AN ANSWER.
COME ON, A REAL FRIEND WOULD DO IT.
REMEMBER, A TRUE FRIEND IS SOMEONE WHO STANDS UP FOR YOU.
LEAVE HER ALONE.

BRILLIANT BOREDOM BUSTERS

ARE ALL YOUR FRIENDS BUSY? HAVE YOU NOTHING TO DO?
DON'T DESPAIR, JUST READ ON.

WHY NOT BUILD YOUR BRAINPOWER? LEARN HOW TO SAY SOMETHING IN FIVE LANGUAGES.

MY BROTHER IS ANNOYING.

MON FRÈRE EST AGAÇANT.

OR LEARN SOMETHING BY HEART.

I WANDERED LONELY AS A CLOUD ...

THIS COULD BE THE DAY TO EARN EXTRA CASH ...

... OR TO LEARN A NEW SKILL.

WHY NOT TRY OUT A NEW HAIRSTYLE?

YOU COULD SORT OUT YOUR CLOTHES.

TOO SMALL.

TOO TATTY.

TA DA!

AND IF YOU MANAGE TO FIND SOME FRIENDS, WHY NOT HAVE A GO AT MAKING YOUR OWN MUSIC VIDEO?

HOW TO SURVIVE TRUTH OR DARE

EVERYONE LOVES A GAME OF TRUTH OR DARE, BUT SOMETIMES IT'S TRICKY TO COME UP WITH GOOD IDEAS ON THE SPOT. HERE ARE SOME SUGGESTIONS FOR DEVILISH DARES TO GIVE YOUR FRIENDS.

1. PUT YOUR CLOTHES ON BACKWARDS AND WEAR THEM TO SCHOOL.

2. TRICK YOUR TASTE BUDS WITH STRANGE FOOD. TRY CEREAL WITH ORANGE JUICE INSTEAD OF MILK.

3. RUN UP TO A BOY YOU DON'T KNOW AND TALK TO HIM.

4. SING YOUR FAVOURITE SONG REALLY LOUDLY INSIDE A SHOP.

5. TAKE YOUR PET PEBBLE FOR A WALK IN THE PARK.

IF TERRIBLE TRUTHS ARE MORE YOUR THING, HERE ARE SOME THAT WILL REVEAL YOUR FRIENDS' INNERMOST SECRETS.

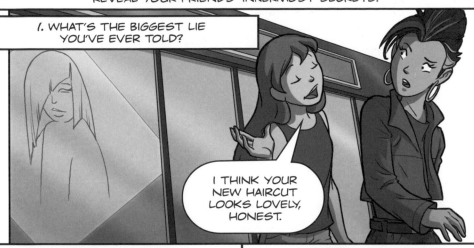

1. WHAT'S THE BIGGEST LIE YOU'VE EVER TOLD?

I THINK YOUR NEW HAIRCUT LOOKS LOVELY, HONEST.

2. WHO IS YOUR SECRET CRUSH?

YOUR BROTHER!

3. WHAT'S THE MOST EMBARRASSING THING THAT HAS HAPPENED TO YOU?

4. WHAT WAS YOUR WEIRDEST DREAM ABOUT?

5. WHAT IS YOUR WORST HABIT?

SO GET READY TO GO AND EMBARRASS YOUR FRIENDS!

HOW TO BEAT BULLIES

BEING BULLIED? DON'T DESPAIR – BULLIES **CAN** BE BEATEN!

BULLIES ARE USUALLY COWARDS WHO PICK ON PEOPLE THEY THINK THEY CAN EASILY UPSET.

1. ALWAYS TELL SOMEONE – IT COULD BE YOUR MUM, A TEACHER, OR ANY ADULT YOU TRUST.

JUST SHARING THE PROBLEM MIGHT MAKE YOU FEEL BETTER ...

THANKS, MUM.

... AND IT'LL GIVE YOU NEW IDEAS FOR HOW TO DEAL WITH IT.

LET'S GO INTO SCHOOL AND TELL THEM WHAT'S BEEN HAPPENING.

2. KEEP A RECORD OF WHAT THE BULLY SAYS AND DOES AND WHEN THEY DO IT.

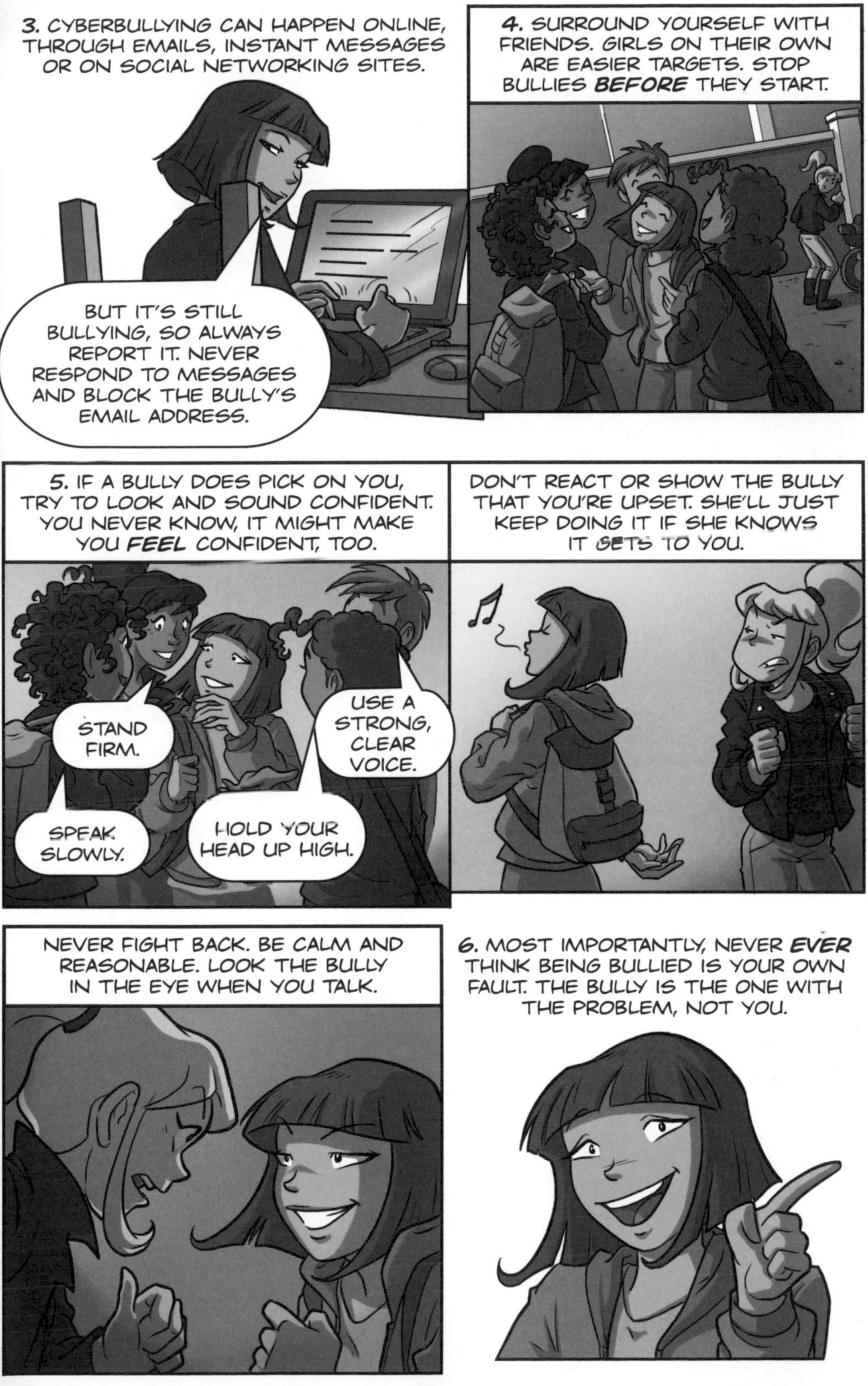
3. CYBERBULLYING CAN HAPPEN ONLINE, THROUGH EMAILS, INSTANT MESSAGES OR ON SOCIAL NETWORKING SITES.
BUT IT'S STILL BULLYING, SO ALWAYS REPORT IT. NEVER RESPOND TO MESSAGES AND BLOCK THE BULLY'S EMAIL ADDRESS.
4. SURROUND YOURSELF WITH FRIENDS. GIRLS ON THEIR OWN ARE EASIER TARGETS. STOP BULLIES ***BEFORE*** THEY START.
5. IF A BULLY DOES PICK ON YOU, TRY TO LOOK AND SOUND CONFIDENT. YOU NEVER KNOW, IT MIGHT MAKE YOU ***FEEL*** CONFIDENT, TOO.
STAND FIRM.
SPEAK SLOWLY.
HOLD YOUR HEAD UP HIGH.
USE A STRONG, CLEAR VOICE.
DON'T REACT OR SHOW THE BULLY THAT YOU'RE UPSET. SHE'LL JUST KEEP DOING IT IF SHE KNOWS IT GETS TO YOU.
NEVER FIGHT BACK. BE CALM AND REASONABLE. LOOK THE BULLY IN THE EYE WHEN YOU TALK.
6. MOST IMPORTANTLY, NEVER ***EVER*** THINK BEING BULLIED IS YOUR OWN FAULT. THE BULLY IS THE ONE WITH THE PROBLEM, NOT YOU.

HOW TO BE A BRILLIANT BABY-SITTER

BABY-SITTING IS A FANTASTIC WAY TO EARN SOME EXTRA MONEY. HERE ARE SOME TIPS TO HELP YOU BECOME THE BEST BABY-SITTER AROUND.

A BRILLIANT BABY-SITTER IS ALWAYS RIGHT ON TIME.

IT'S A GOOD IDEA TO TIRE OUT THE KIDS BEFORE BEDTIME.

IT'S IMPORTANT TO ASK THE PARENTS SOME QUESTIONS BEFORE THEY GO OUT ...

DO THEY NEED SNACKS?

WHAT TIME DO THEY GO TO BED?

HOW CAN I CONTACT YOU?

... BECAUSE SMALL CHILDREN HAVE BEEN KNOWN TO EXAGGERATE.

MUM LETS US STAY UP UNTIL TEN.

WE EAT SWEETS IN BED.

BUT REMEMBER TO CALM THINGS DOWN BEFORE BED OR THEY'LL NEVER GO TO SLEEP.

WHEN BEDTIME COMES, BE FIRM ...

... BUT KIND.

I'LL LEAVE THE LANDING LIGHT ON.

YES, YOU **DO** HAVE TO BRUSH YOUR TEETH.

BABY-SITTING CAN BE A GOOD TIME TO CATCH UP ON HOMEWORK.

BUT DON'T COUNT ON IT. SOMETIMES THINGS JUST DON'T WORK OUT AS PLANNED.

NEVER IGNORE A PROBLEM. IT WON'T GO AWAY!

INSTEAD, TRY TO FIND A WAY TO SOLVE IT.

FLUFFY WANTS TO SLEEP NOW, JACK.

BECOME A BRILLIANT BABY-SITTER AND YOU'LL NEVER BE SHORT OF JOBS!

Also Available:

**Girls' World
Doodling and Colouring**
ISBN: 978-1-907151-45-3

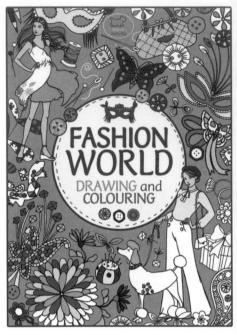

**Fashion World
Drawing and Colouring**
ISBN: 978-1-78055-011-4

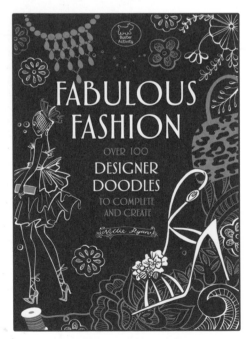

Fabulous Fashion
ISBN: 978-1-907151-84-2

The Girls' Handbook
ISBN: 978-1-907151-12-5